STANIER PACIFICS

DEREK HUNTRISS

IAN ALLAN
Publishing

Front cover:
Immaculate 'Coronation' class Pacific No 46240 *City of Coventry* is bathed in afternoon sunlight as it rests between duties outside Willesden (1A) MPD in February 1964. *R. Hobbs*

Rear cover:
'Princess Royal' No 46207 *Princess Arthur of Connaught* takes water from Castlethorpe troughs as it heads up the 'Merseyside Express' on 30 August 1958. *T. B. Owen*

This page:
No 46240 receives last minute attention at Camden MPD on 29 June 1962 before taking the Royal train from Euston later that evening. *G. Rixon*

INTRODUCTION

First published 1993

ISBN 0 7110 2068 X

Published by Ian Allan Ltd, Shepperton, Surrey; and printed by Ian Allan Printing Ltd at their works at Coombelands in Runnymede, England.

In 1932, the LMS owned no locomotives capable of working a 500-ton express single handed throughout the 401 mile journey from London Euston to Glasgow Central. Appointed as Chief Mechanical Engineer on 1 January 1932, William Stanier's remit was to produce a design to meet that requirement. Three prototype Pacifics were included in the construction programme, although the third was held back and was eventually completed as the turbine-driven No 6202 *Turbomotive*. No 6200 *The Princess Royal* was completed by 27 June 1933 and, of course, William Stanier must take the credit. Between 1933 and 1937, he was responsible for producing the entire range of standard locomotives that came to serve the LMS so well: 'Princesses', 'Coronations', 'Jubilees', 'Black Fives', '8F' 2-8-0s and the various classes of passenger tanks.

The genesis, life and times of Stanier's Pacifics have been well documented over many years, probably in more detail than any other class of steam locomotive and it is not the author's intention to add to the historical arguments, but rather to provide the reader with an excellent selection of pictures, mainly taken when the Pacifics were in everyday service. They have been arranged in geographical order to represent a journey from London Euston to Glasgow

Right:
On a clear Summer afternoon in June 1959, No 46224 Princess Alexandra heads an up express south of Leyland.
P. Hughes

Left:
No 46235 *City of Birmingham* is being serviced on Willesden (1A) MPD before returning north with a Rugby Cup Final special on 11 May 1963. Withdrawn from traffic in October 1964, No 46235 was stored at Nuneaton (2B) MPD from January to December 1965. After undergoing five months' restoration at Crewe Works, No 46235 was delivered by low loader to the City of Birmingham Science Museum on Sunday 22 May 1966 where it has been immured ever since.
G. Rixon

Central with visits to MPDs, works and lineside locations. Following this journey, other regular haunts of the Pacifics are visited including Shrewsbury, Llandudno Junction, Runcorn and Perth. Late in their lives, the Pacifics were used for railtour duties on regions away from the LMS and their usual routes: pictures taken at Swindon, Skipton, Leeds and Derby are amongst those included. Finally we see examples of both 'Princess Royal' and 'Coronation' classes in store before their final journeys to the scrap-yard. As time has moved on, examples of both classes have been preserved, and a picture of No 46229 *Duchess of Hamilton* making its first run in preservation has been included.

Having recalled the everyday workings of the LMS 'Pacifics', Stanier's design masterpiece, thanks must be offered to all the dedicated photographers whose irreplaceable images provide the contents of this book. Without their efforts, this title would not have been possible.

Derek Huntriss
Camborne, Cornwall

December 1992

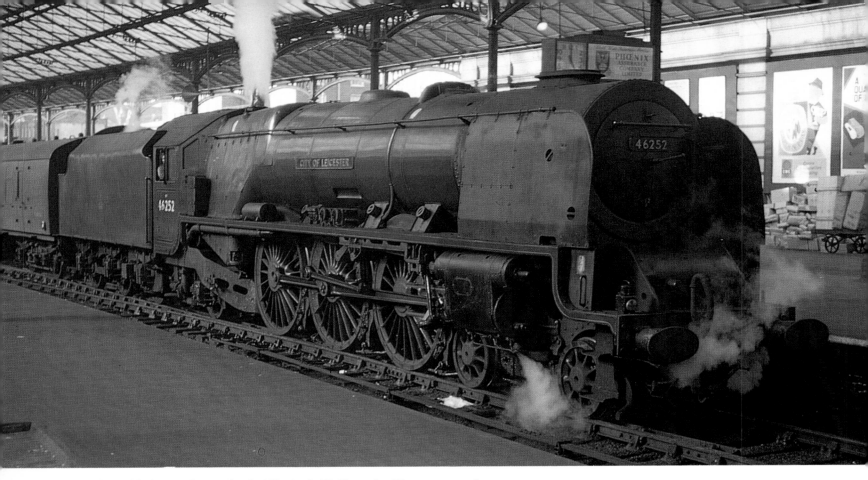

No 46252 *City of Leicester* **has arrived at Euston's Platform 1 with an express from Holyhead in July 1962. Built close to the site where Trevithick demonstrated his 'Catch-Me-Who-Can' in 1808, Hardwick's Euston station was opened on Thursday 20 July 1837. Over the years, piecemeal additions were made to accommodate heavier traffic and longer trains. After surviving several schemes for rebuilding, the old Euston finally succumbed in 1965, when it was in the throes of reconstruction. The rebuilt station was opened on 14 October 1968 by Her Majesty the Queen, who during her speech proclaimed 'This opening marks the the completion of the most important railway modernisation project of this century'.**
G. Rixon

Allocated to Camden (1B) MPD for most of its working life, No 46239 *City of Chester* awaits departure from Euston with the 4.45pm to Liverpool Lime Street on 27 July 1962. After subsequent reallocations to Willesden (1A) and Crewe North (5A) MPDs in 1963 and 1964 respectively, No 46239 was withdrawn from the latter depot in October 1964, when it was placed in store for two months before despatch to Cashmore's scrapyard at Great Bridge for breaking up. *G. Rixon*

Left:
A classic portrait of No 46240 *City of Coventry* ready for its next turn of duty at Camden (1B) MPD in July 1963. Camden was fortunate in having a modern ash plant on which the mountains of hot ash could be expeditiously removed in one of the plant's narrow gauge trucks, an example of which can be seen adjacent to the locomotive's firebox. After completing the highest mileage of all the Stanier Pacifics — 1,685,000 — No 46240 was withdrawn in October 1964 and was scrapped in Cashmore's yard at Great Bridge in December of that year. The only items from *City of Coventry* that survive are its nameplates, crests and smokebox door numberplate, one set adorning the rebuilt Coventry station and the other in private ownership. The smokebox door numberplate displayed at Coventry station is one of 20 cast at the Coventry plant of Morris Engines by a colleague of the author. *P. Riley courtesy N. Simms*

Above:
Showing the earlier BR-style livery with the lining set in from the panel edges, a livery which was also used for locomotives carrying the blue and green liveries, No 46225 *Duchess of Gloucester* waits to move onto Camden shed on 1 February 1959. *T. B. Owen*

Carrying BR's later LMS-style livery with the lining at the panel edges, No 46238 *City of Carlisle* is being turned on Camden's 70ft vacuum-operated turntable before being switched to the appropriate shed road. The only basic change from the original LMS livery was the use of yellow lines instead of the gold and vermilion lines that were applied to Nos 6230-6234. This is an August 1962 picture.
G. Rixon

One of five 'Princess Royals' to receive BR red livery during the course of 1958, the nameplate and motion of No 46208 *Princess Helena Victoria* were photographed at Camden in February 1959. Following initial withdrawal of the class in March 1961, No 46208 was one of six members of the class to be temporarily returned to traffic for the summer 1962 timetable. Amongst other duties, No 46208 was employed on the sparse Euston-Birmingham-Wolverhampton services. However, the reprieve was to be shortlived as No 46208 was withdrawn by October 1962 and following short periods in store at Camden MPD and Crewe Works, she had been broken up by November of that year. *T. B. Owen*

Top left:
With little room for laid up engines at Camden MPD, No 46207 *Princess Arthur of Connaught* is groomed for Winter storage outside Willesden MPD on 25 March 1961. Along with all other member of the class, she had been withdrawn from traffic that month. After operation during the 1961 summer timetable, No 46207 was returned to store at Willesden together with No 46205 *Princess Helena Victoria*. Both were condemned in November 1961.
T. B. Owen

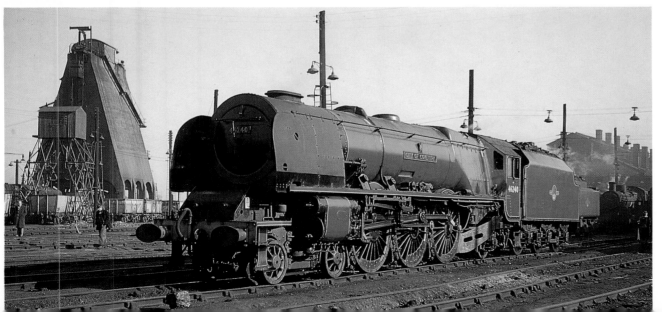

Bottom left:
Photographed at Willesden MPD on 8 March 1964, No 46240 *City of Coventry* was one of the last locomotives to leave Camden depot before it closed to steam from 9 September 1963. No 46240 was one of the final batch of Stanier Pacifics to be withdrawn in September 1964, receiving the diagonal yellow restrictive stripes on her cabsides only days before withdrawal.
N. Fields

Left:
A gleaming No 46239 *City of Chester* catches the afternoon sunlight inside the roundhouse at Willesden (1A) MPD on 14 September 1963. Alongside was the immaculate No 46245 *City of London*, both locomotives being kept in excellent condition for standby duties. *G. Rixon*

Above:
This picture of No 46242 *City of Glasgow* taken on 31 May 1960, captures the atmosphere outside the shed at Willesden (1A). Often dubbed 'The Old Grey Lady of the London Midland', Willesden was often host to over 100 engines, some invariably priming the north west London air with coal tar and adding to the gritty fumes from the nearby Acton Lane power station. It wasn't difficult to see how 'Willesden Grey Livery' got its name. *G. Rixon*

Above:
A classic action shot of an LMS 'Coronation' Pacific hauling a near complete rake of ex-LMS stock — No 46254 *City of Stoke on Trent* heads north through Bushey station in July 1963. From the train, the whole 158 miles of the old LNWR main line from Euston to Crewe appears to be a well graded romp through rolling country side with the odd small market town in its path. However, in reality, whilst the southern section with its gently sweeping curves fits this description, the section between Rugby and Stafford twists more severely, particularly round the mining areas of the South Staffordshire coalfield.
P. Riley

Right:
Depicted previously in this title at Willesden MPD, also on 11 May 1963, No 46235 *City of Birmingham* heads 1Z57, an up special for Wembley, near Berkhamsted. Today's overhead catenary obscure vantage points for photographers, whereas this picture illustrates the problems posed by endless miles of telegraph poles in years gone by.
T. B. Owen

Left:
**With the progress of forthcoming
electrification well evident in this picture,
No 46228 *Duchess of Rutland* speeds past
Hillmorton box with a down Perth express on
17 August 1963. Allocated to Crewe North
(5A) MPD from October 1957, No 46228
survived at that depot until its withdrawal in
October 1964. After only one month in store
at its home shed, it was despatched to
Cashmore's scrap yard at Great Bridge where
it met the cutter's torch in December of that
year.** *J. N. Simms*

Above:
**One week later, on 24 August 1963,
No 46257 *City of Salford* passes Hillmorton
with an up express. The only BR built
'Duchess', No 46257 was identical to
No 6256 and entered traffic on 19 May 1948.
Officially named by the Lord Mayor of Salford
at a ceremony on 3 June 1948 at Manchester
Exchange station, No 46257 was returned to
Crewe Works for a further 18 days where it
was observed with its trailing truck removed.**
J. N. Simms

No 46234 *Duchess of Abercorn* is an unusual visitor to Rugby MPD on 23 August 1959. With its trailing axlebox cover removed, it could be assumed that it had failed in traffic with a hot box and was awaiting repair. One of the early victims of the Modernisation Plan, No 46234 was withdrawn in January 1963 and after a brief period in store at Carlisle Upperby (12B) MPD, was broken up at Crewe Works in June 1963.

Considered by some as the prime example of Stanier 'Coronation' class Pacific to be preserved, No 46234 was the first member of the class to be fitted with a double blastpipe and chimney. On 26 February 1939, No 6234 was selected by the LMS to haul a test train consisting of 20 coaches, weighing 610 tons, on a return trip between Crewe and Glasgow. A schedule of 150min was set up for the 141 mile journey from Crewe to Carlisle which included the ascent of Shap and the remaining 102.3 miles from Carlisle to Glasgow Central, over Beattock, was to be completed in 118min. In the event, No 6234 placed herself in the history books by exerting 3,300hp at the cylinders, a record for any British steam locomotive. Having met the schedules for the outward trip and with only a two hour servicing stop in Glasgow, No 6234 set about the return to Crewe covering a total of 487 miles under normal service conditions. *T. B. Owen*

By 1963, the introduction of the English Electric Type 4 diesels meant that the 'Coronation' class Pacifics lost many of their top link passenger duties and were often to be found hauling express freight workings. Here, No 46225 *Duchess of Gloucester* is approaching Brinklow with an up fitted goods on 16 March 1963. One of 16 'Coronation' class Pacifics to receive the BR red livery, No 46225 was one of the last survivors of the class to remain in traffic, acquiring the yellow cab-side warning stripe denoting its prohibition from working under the energised wires south of Crewe in 1964. Withdrawn from Carlisle Upperby (12B) MPD in October 1964, No 46225 remained in store for two months before despatch to the West of Scotland Shipbreaking Co at Troon where it was scrapped together with seven other members of the class. *J. N. Simms*

Left:
Super power for the up 'Red Rose' as it leaves Crewe behind No 46256 *Sir William A. Stanier F.R.S.* and an unidentified 'Royal Scot' in August 1958. At that time there were few signs of the impending electrification of the West Coast main line. Two years later, Stage 1 of the London Midland Region's 25kV electrification programme was complete with the inauguration of electric traction between Crewe and Manchester on 12 September 1960. In this view of No 46256, can be see the wiring to the electric headlamps, a feature which had been removed before the locomotive was withdrawn in October 1964.
M. S. Welch

Above:
A superb study of No 46228 *Duchess of Rutland* as she waits at Crewe to take the up 'Midday Scot' forward to Euston in August 1958. Allocated to Crewe North (5A) MPD in October 1957, No 46228 was to remain at that depot until withdrawal came in October 1964. After only one month in store at Crewe North, she was towed to Cashmore's Great Bridge scrap-yard where she was broken up, it was felt with indecent haste. *M. S. Welch*

Above:
Fresh from the works, and awaiting its first firing after overhaul, No 46232 *Duchess of Montrose* stands in Crewe Works paintshop yard in May 1959. Following initial allocation to Camden in July 1938, No 46232 was reallocated to Glasgow Polmadie (66A) MPD in 1940, where she remained for the rest of her working life. *P. Hughes*

Right:
Having received its full cylindrical smokebox on its previous visit to Crewe Works in March 1957, No 46239 *City of Chester* stands outside the Paint Shop in May 1959. Built at a cost of £10,838 in August 1939, No 46239 was allocated to Camden (1B) MPD where it worked until closure of that depot in September 1963. A 12-month allocation to

Willesden (1A) MPD followed before No 46239 was transferred to Crewe North (5A) MPD in August 1964. After only two months' operating from Crewe North, No 46239 was withdrawn in October 1964 and was despatched to Cashmore's Great Bridge scrap yard where it joined eight other members of the class in their final resting place. *P. Hughes*

This unusual rear view taken at Crewe station shows No 46235 *City of Birmingham* and No 46251 *City of Nottingham* as they change over whilst working the up 'Midday Scot' in August 1958. No 46251 was to receive the newly introduced BR red livery some three months later, in November 1958. *M. S. Welch*

Above right:
Electrification at Crewe station is well in evidence in this view taken five years later in June 1963 as No 46242 *City of Glasgow* waits to depart with an up working. Always a Mecca for visiting and local trainspotters, the platforms at Crewe would reverberate the dulcet tones of the station announcer proclaiming: 'This is Crewe, Crewe station, Crewe' — as if anybody really needed reminding. Whether this style of announcement was BR corporate policy or just one particular lady announcer's style will probably never be known, but the author can well recall the same tones proclaiming; 'This is Carlisle, Carlisle station, Carlisle'. *N. Fields*

Below right:
Having worked the RCTS 'Scottish Lowlander' railtour on the previous day, No 46256 *Sir William A. Stanier F.R.S.* has just enough steam left to move forward out of Crewe North (5A) MPD on 26 September 1964, to make what was the last movement of a 'Coronation' class Pacific in BR service. *N. Fields*

Built as the penultimate member of the 'Princess Royal' class in September 1935 and named after the Queen of Norway, No 46211 *Queen Maud* is depicted outside the Paint Shop at Crewe works in May 1959. Initially allocated to Camden (1B) MPD when new, No 46211 had been reallocated by January 1948 to Crewe North (5A) MPD, a depot which was to be its home until November 1959 when it was transferred to Liverpool Edge Hill (8A) MPD. Following several months allocation to Carnforth (24L) MPD from March 1961, No 46211 returned to Crewe North (5A) MPD in July 1961, where it became one of the first members of the class to be withdrawn from service in October 1961. *P. Hughes*

Left:
Carrying the earlier BR-style yellow and black lining set in from the edge of the panels, a feature which the locomotive received on a visit to Crewe Works in July 1957, No 46240 *City of Coventry* **heads a down express near Winsford on a clear Summer day in June 1959.** *P. Hughes*

Above:
Easily distinguished by the heavy outside motion brackets, No 46205 *Princess Victoria* **heads an up express near Winsford in June 1959. This rather ugly feature was the result of an experiment which took place c1946/7 when she had her two inside sets of Walschaerts valve motion removed and rocking levers fitted. Whether this modification made any appreciable difference to her performance is debatable, although contemporary reports suggested she became a rough rider and in 1955 the original Walschaerts valve motion was restored although the heavy outside motion brackets remained until the end of her days.** *P. Hughes*

This pleasing picture of No 46252 *City of Leicester* heading an up express near Leyland was taken in June 1959. Together with No 6232, No 6252 was the first 'Coronation' to be fitted with smoke deflectors in March 1945; No 6253 and subsequent members of the class carried them from new. There were two basic types of deflector plate fitted to members of this class dependent on whether they had a continuous footplate or not. Those which did (Nos 6230-4, 46242 and 6249-52) had the lower front end of the plate extended downwards below the drop in level to the front buffer beam, whilst the remainder had the bottom front edge of the plates level with the main footplate. Allocated to Crewe North (5A) MPD for the majority of its working life, No 46252 amassed a total of 1,231,032 miles before its withdrawal from traffic in June 1963. *P. Hughes*

With a clear chimney, No 46236 *City of Bradford* makes light work with an up express as it climbs the 1 in 106 gradient towards Farington Junction, south of Preston, in July 1961. Following Nationalisation in 1948, No 46236 was selected for an exchange of locomotives between the different regions. During the course of these trials the locomotives involved burned the same coal and were driven by their own crews in an attempt to obtain a meaningful set of results. Tested initially for a period of five days in April 1948 over its own main line, No 46236 hauled the down 'Royal Scot' from Euston to Carlisle on one day, returning on the next with the 12.55pm from Carlisle. Next, No 46236 worked over the Eastern Region between King's Cross and Leeds, followed by a period on the Western Region where it was used between Paddington and Plymouth over the formidable South Devon banks. Finally, after an interval of three weeks during which No 46236 had been fitted with an ex-WD tender, tests resumed over the Southern Region when it handled the 'Atlantic Coast Express' between Waterloo and Exeter. The extra capacity of the ex-WD tender compensated for the lack of water troughs on the Southern Region of BR. *P. Hughes*

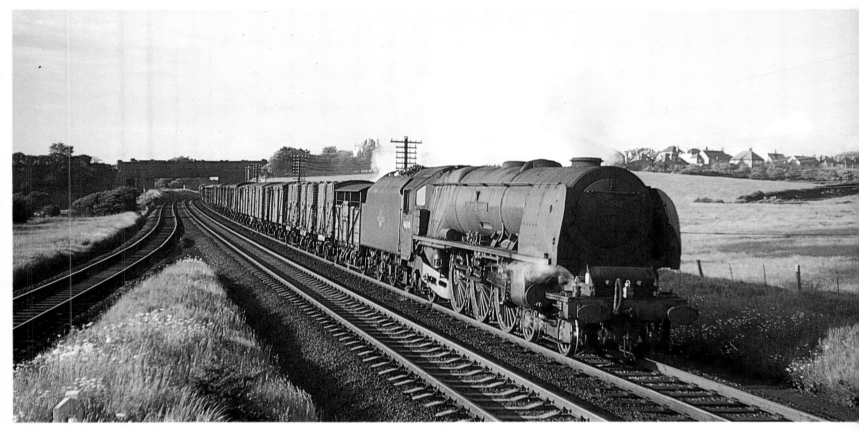

Unkempt, careworn, and in its last weeks of operational service, No 46208 *Princess Helena Victoria* waits to take over the 12.50pm from Barrow to Euston at the south end of Preston station on Sunday 19 August 1962. Then allocated to Liverpool Edge Hill (8A) MPD, No 46208 had been serviced at Lostock Hall (24C) MPD prior to working this train which was usually booked for 'Duchess' haulage. It was contemplated that the

'Princess Royals' could have had an extended life on freight traffic, but this proved to be impractical, their wheelbase being too long for the curves in some of the major freight yards including Willesden and Carlisle Kingmoor. *P. Fitton*

Above:
Many of their top link passenger duties handed over to the new English Electric Type 4 diesels, the 'Duchesses' were found alternative work hauling express freight turns. Here, No 46240 *City of Coventry* was photographed south of Hest Bank with the 2.4pm Carlisle-Broad Street freight on 5 June 1964. The line to Morecambe and Heysham can be seen forking to the left of the picture. *D. A. Codling*

Above:
No 46246 *City of Manchester* coasts down the last mile of 1 in 146 into Tebay with an up working in September 1961. No 46246 was the last member of the class to lose its sloping smokebox top in May 1960, and was among the first of the class to be withdrawn in June 1963. *P. Hughes*

Right:
Today, the only example of 'Coronation' class Pacific to see main line use, No 46229 *Duchess of Hamilton* is depicted under very different circumstances on 1 June 1957. Carrying a very work-stained green livery, No 46229 is working an up express at Yanwath, south of Penrith. Only weeks before, No 46229 had been chosen to head the up working of the inaugural run of the newly introduced high speed 'Caledonian Express'. After withdrawal from BR service in February 1964, No 46229 survived the cutter's torch thanks to Butlins Ltd, who acquired it to be displayed outside their holiday camp at Minehead, where it remained until 1975 when it was placed on loan to the National Railway Museum. The locomotive was restored to main line running condition at the museum. *T. B. Owen*

A classic portrait of No 46238 *City of Carlisle* as it stands outside its namesake depot at Carlisle Upperby (12B) on 13 June 1964. At that time No 46238 was used mainly for standby duties in case of diesel failures and was withdrawn from service only four months later, in October. After one month in store at Upperby, No 46238 was towed to the West of Scotland Shipbreaking Co at Troon, where it joined seven other members of the class for breaking up. *N. Fields*

The familiar lines of Carlisle Upperby's roundhouse are the backdrop for this picture of No 46225 *Duchess of Gloucester* in July 1964. Together with No 46238, the locomotive's main task was as standby for the English Electric Type 4 diesels, whose availability was plagued by mechanical problems which ensured that the 'Duchesses' were still very much part of the West Coast main line scene until the late Summer of 1964.
G. Morrison

Left:
Pictured at Carlisle Upperby (12B) MPD on 30 August 1964, No 46237 *City of Bristol* is carrying the distinctive yellow stripe on its cab-side banning its use under overhead electrified wires. No 46200 *The Princess Royal* can be seen in store behind a line of trucks. The last member of the class to be withdrawn from traffic in November 1962, No 46200 had seen storage at Carlisle Kingmoor (12A) MPD and was despatched to Connell's scrap-yard at Coatbridge for breaking up in September 1964. *N. Fields*

Above:
No 46201 *Princess Elizabeth* awaits departure from Carlisle Citadel's Platform 4 with an up Glasgow to Birmingham express on 9 June 1960. Alongside, Stanier Class 5 No 45131 pilots another member of the class with an up working. Carlisle Citadel's classic overall roof and ornamental screen were removed during 1957-58 as were the London North Western Railway signals.
T. B. Owen

Left:
**Like sister locomotive
No 46330 *Duchess of
Buccleuch*, No 46231
Duchess of Atholl was a
lifetime Polmadie (66A)
MPD engine. Here,
No 46231 is shown
outside Carlisle
Kingmoor (12A) MPD on
14 August 1960. In the
late 1940s, No 46231
was the choice for a
superb Hornby-Dublo
model which cost the
then princely sum of £10
for the set — a small**

Above:
Formally withdrawn from traffic on 12 October 1964, No 46256 *Sir William A. Stanier F.R.S.* **was reinstated to work the RCTS 'Scottish Lowlander' railtour on 26 October 1964. Pictured here alongside Carlisle No 4 signalbox, No 46256 had just completed the first northbound leg. The return by No 46256 from Carlisle to Crewe marked the last operational working of the class in BR service.** *N. Fields*

Bottom right:
This detail view of Pacifics No 46247 *City of Liverpool* **in maroon and No 46242** *City of Glasgow* **in green livery, clearly shows the detail difference in the front ends of the rebuilt streamlined locomotives and those built without streamlining. However, No 46242 was the exception to the general rule in that she was given a continuous footplate following the Harrow disaster. No 46247 does not have the graceful curved plate of Nos 46230-4 and Nos 46249-52, the locomotives which had been de-streamlined.** *G. W. Morrison*

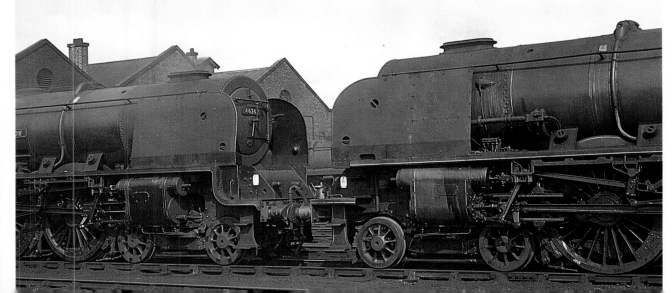

Top left:

Just six weeks before withdrawal, No 46203 *Princess Margaret Rose* **backs down off Carlisle Kingmoor (12A) MPD on 29 August 1962, to take over the 10.00am Euston-Perth, a train normally diesel hauled north of Crewe. Declared surplus to requirements and withdrawn from traffic, No 46203 had only covered 6,000+ miles since an intermediate repair at Crewe Works and arrived in preservation in excellent mechanical condition complete with all her fittings. Purchased by Mr (later Sir) Billy Butlin for display at his company's Pwllheli holiday camp in North Wales, No 46203 was repainted in LMS livery at Crewe Works before despatch to her new home in May 1963. After a number of years' exposure to salt-laden air, her external condition deteriorated and Butlins approached David Ward, the then British Rail manager for steam operations on BR, for advice regarding a suitable home. The Midland Railway Centre at Butterley was chosen on the condition that the Centre paid the cost of transportation from Pwllheli to Butterley.**
P. Fitton

Climbing the 1 in 74 towards Beattock summit at
Harthope, No 46247 *City of Liverpool* is seen at the head
of the down 'Royal Scot' in May 1960. One year later,
No 46247 was transferred from Camden (1B) MPD to
Carlisle Kingmoor (12A) MPD where she remained
allocated until withdrawn in June 1963. *G. W. Morrison*

Photographed crossing Braidhurst viaduct, one half mile north of Motherwell station on the line to Perth, No 46224 *Princess Alexandra* is heading a lightweight, Sundays only, Perth-Carstairs train in June 1960. Built as the last of the blue streamliners, No 6224 spent two years allocated to Camden (1B) MPD when built and was reallocated to Glasgow Polmadie (66A) in late 1939, where she remained until withdrawn from traffic in October 1963. One of 13 members of the class to be withdrawn that year, No 46224 was despatched to Crewe Works immediately after withdrawal to be broken up 'At Home'. *E. Aitchison*

Allocated to Camden (1B) MPD, No 46242 *City of Glasgow* is pictured outside Glasgow Polmadie (66A) MPD on 2 June 1957. Some four years later, in March 1961, No 46242 was reallocated to her namesake depot at Glasgow Polmadie where she remained for the rest of her working life. No 46242 had the distinction of hauling the inaugural down run of the 'Caledonian Express' in June 1957.

This train was the nearest BR ever came to emulating the prewar 'Coronation Scot'. The accelerated timing of 7¼hr between London Euston and Glasgow for this newly introduced express was achieved at the cost of rigidly restricting the formation to eight coaches leaving second-class passengers with the discomfort of sitting four abreast in open coaches. Seats had to be booked in advance,

since no standing was permitted, which often meant that passengers with no reservation were left behind. *T. B. Owen*

This 1959 picture shows No 46201 *Princess Elizabeth* about to depart from Glasgow Central with an up express. Withdrawn from revenue earning service on BR in October 1961, No 46201 was offered to the founder members of the 6201 Princess Elizabeth Preservation Society for £2,160 on the condition that the locomotive be kept at a suitable site. Initially, three sites were considered, Haworth on the Keighley and Worth Valley Railway, Hednesford, and the Railway Preservation Society site at Ashchurch; the last named being the eventual destination for No 46201. Making its own way in steam from Carlisle via Leeds to Saltley, where the fire was dropped, No 46201 had its motion taken down before being towed by diesel to Ashchurch. Several years of effort by members were rewarded on Whit Sunday 1965 when *Princess Elizabeth* was returned to steam once more. However, it was to be many years later before No 6201 returned to main line running, but eventually — on 24 April 1976 — she deputised for No 6000 *King George V* and began her first railtour in preservation. *The late B. J. Swain/Colour Rail*

These two pictures, taken in July 1963, depict No 46238 *City of Carlisle* at Shrewsbury, a destination often visited by 'Coronation' class locomotives running-in or building up mileage prior to entering works. One of the regular return diagrams from Shrewsbury back to Crewe was the 8.00am Newquay-Manchester. The picture opposite shows No 46238 under an impressive array of Western Region signals as an unidentified GWR 'Hall' class 4-6-0 enters the station.
Both: D. Penney

Right:
Whilst the Stanier Pacifics were primarily to be found on duties along the West Coast main line, they could also be seen at Liverpool, Shrewsbury, Perth, Glasgow St Enoch and on the Holyhead boat trains along the North Wales coast. This picture shows prototype Stanier Pacific No 46200 *The Princess Royal* **arriving at Llandudno Junction with an RCTS special in June 1962.** *D. Penney*

Far right:
The RCTS special having been taken forward to Llandudno by two 2-6-4Ts, No 46200 is depicted outside Llandudno Junction (6G) MPD in the final red livery given to four members of the class (along with 16 'Duchesses') from 1957 onwards. *D. Penney*

Far left:
This classic study portrays No 46211 *Queen Maud* departing from the seldom photographed station at Runcorn with a Liverpool-Euston express in June 1959. Together with five of her classmates, No 46211 was allocated to Liverpool Edge Hill MPD and was used for fast express work from Liverpool to Euston and Glasgow. It was reputed in northern circles that the Edge Hill crews had the 'Princesses' weighed up far better than any other on the LM Region, and could drive them better too — but doubtless the men of Camden and Crewe would have something to say about that. By the end of 1960 four 'Duchesses' had been drafted in to replace the 'Princesses' as they were displaced to other MPDs for a short time prior to withdrawal, although No 46208 *Princess Helena Victoria* remained at 8A until final withdrawal in October 1962.
D. Penney

Left:
Allocated to Carlisle Kingmoor (12A) MPD in March 1961, No 46255 *City of Hereford* is working an up parcels south of Hilton Junction, Perth in July 1963. A Carlisle locomotive for most of her working life, No 46255 was among the last batch of 'Duchesses' to be withdrawn in October 1964. *P. Hughes*

Top right:

Carrying the BR green livery which it received in February 1952, No 46252 *City of Leicester* poses under the coaling stage at Perth (63A) MPD in May 1960. Outshopped from Crewe Works on 24 June 1944 for a total cost of £11,664, No 46252 spent most of its working life being allocated to depots outside the London area, its first six years being allocated to Crewe North (5A) MPD. One of the first examples of the class to be withdrawn in June 1963, No 46252 had amassed a total of 1,231,032 miles on its record card. *The late W. J. V. Anderson/Colour-Rail*

Bottom right:

Having arrived at Perth with a down working, No 46257 *City of Salford* awaits access to Perth MPD, in May 1964. Built during H. G. Ivatt's two-year spell (1945-47) as the LMS railway's Chief Mechanical Engineer, No 46257 was the only 'Duchess' to enter traffic under BR. Identical twin to No 6256, *City of Salford* incorporated detail modifications including modified rear trucks, roller bearings and other mechanical variations. The last two 'Duchesses' were easily recognisable by their shortened cab side sheets. *D. Penney*

On its final day in BR service, No 46256 *Sir William A. Stanier F.R.S.* is seen climbing towards Shap summit with the RCTS 'Scottish Lowlander' Railtour on 26 October 1964. On reaching Carlisle, No 46256 was replaced by LNER 'A4' 4-6-2 No 60007 *Sir Nigel Gresley* for the run to Edinburgh over the Waverley route.
T. B. Owen

An unusual venue for a Stanier Pacific — No 46238 *City of Carlisle* waits at Skipton (24G) MPD before working the SLS/RCTS 'North Eastern Railtour' over the Settle and Carlisle route on 27 September 1963. The tour arrived in Skipton from Harrogate via the Ilkley-Otley line behind LMS '4F' No 44467. Alongside No 46238 is LMS 'Jinty' No 47454.
P. Fitton

Above:

Gleaming in the late afternoon sunlight outside Swindon (82C) MPD, No 46251 *City of Nottingham* had arrived with the RCTS 'East Midlander' railtour from Nottingham. The tour, which visited both Eastleigh and Swindon Works, had traversed the Great Central route via Woodford Halse. No 46251 was replaced at Didcot for the run over the Didcot, Newbury & Southampton line to Eastleigh by Bulleid Pacific No 34038 *Lynton*. *R. Hobbs*

Right:

Here, No 46247 *City of Liverpool* awaits departure from Leeds City with an earlier railtour over the Settle and Carlisle on 9 July 1961. This was not the first occasion that a Stanier Pacific had worked over the S&C. In the third week of March 1956, No 46225 *Duchess of Gloucester* was employed, for the first time on record, but not in revenue earning service, over the S&C. No 46225 was following its recent tests on the Rugby test plant with road work between Carlisle and Skipton. Mobile test units were employed and the Pacific was seen hauling loads of up to 20 bogies. *T. B. Owen*

Exhibition duty — No 46245 *City of London,* adorned with the yellow cab-side restrictive stripe, is at Derby Works' open day on 29 August 1964. Other exhibits included 2-6-4 tank No 42500, which was scheduled for preservation, and former Southern diesel-electric locomotives Nos 10201 and 10203 which were in store.
N. Fields

Photographed climbing the 1 in 200 of Gamston bank, No 46245 *City of London* was working the return leg of a railtour up the East Coast main line from Doncaster to King's Cross on 9 June 1963. Contrary to a claim made by the Lord Mayor of London, the Hon Sir Peter Vanneck, when he named Class 87 electric No 87005 *City of London* on 22 November 1978, he was not the first Lord Mayor of London to name a locomotive. LMS streamline Pacific, No 6245, painted in wartime unlined black livery, was named *City of London* by one of his predecessors, Sir Samuel G. Joseph, at a ceremony at Euston Station on 20 July 1943. *D. Penney*

Left:
**Duties no more — the last 'Princess Royal' to be
withdrawn from traffic in November 1962, No 46200 *The
Princess Royal* is depicted outside Carlisle Upperby
(12B) MPD in September 1963.** *G. Rixon*

Above:
**Shorn of its nameplates, No 46246 *City of Manchester* is
seen in store outside Camden (1B) MPD on 2 February
1963, only one month after official withdrawal. No 46246
was to remain at Camden until April 1963 when it was
towed to Crewe Works for scrapping. Officially
completing 1,168,596 miles in traffic until records
ceased to be kept in 1959, No 46246 held the distinction
of being one of eight members of the class to average
over 70,000 miles per year in revenue earning service.** *G.
Rixon*

'Duchess' reincarnate. Almost 16 years after No 46256 had made her final journey over Shap in October 1964, preserved 'Coronation' No 46229 *Duchess of Hamilton* makes an impressive return to steam as she leaves York with the first 'Limited Edition' railtour on Saturday 10 May 1980. Steam leakages from the cylinder drain cocks and pressure relief valves were to prove a recurring problem and it was to be more than a year later on 11 November 1981 when No 46229 hauled the 'Postal Special' that the front end was finally steam tight.
D. Huntriss